Dedicated to Sophia

This is a book about frogs...

And tadpoles too!

They'll be waking up soon...

Spring

And making their debut!

Frogs live in ponds all year round.

I didn't know that! Did you?

And most frogs hibernate in winter...

Which means they sleep their way through!

Since frogs don't migrate like birds and mammals...

I wonder why, don't you?

It's because they are amphibians.

I couldn't hop that far, could you?

When frogs sleep in the winter their body freezes...

Even though they are still alive...

Frogs are amazing - how they adapt to winter!

They have learned how to help their species survive

And now it's time to JUMP JUMP JUMP...

And RIBBIT, RIBBIT, RIBBIT LIKE A FROG!

Frogs lay eggs in the spring...

The survivors turn into tadpoles...

But first the eggs must avoid natural enemies...

Like herons, ducks, snakes and crows.

Frogs like us have two eyes...

But they see quite well in the dark at night.

Yes, frogs have excellent twenty four hour vision!

As nocturals they are out of sight!

Like us, they avoid too much sunlight...

Which is why we might see only their heads popping up...

As they nab a flea or fly to sup!

Like us, frogs need water...

But they drink it in through their skin...

Tree frogs are not the same...

They soak up rain from the trees they live in.

And now it's time to JUMP JUMP JUMP

And RIBBIT, RIBBIT, RIBBIT LIKE A FROG!

Not all frogs say RIBBIT...

But the sound is fun to do!

So, let's make it one last time!

I hope you'll join in too!

Let's JUMP JUMP JUMP

And RIBBIT, RIBBIT, RIBBIT LIKE A FROG!

WE

FROG
RIBBITS!

Jump Series:

Jump Like a Caribou!
Jump Like a Kangaroo!
Jump at the Zoo!
Jump and Say P.U.!
Jump and Say Boo!
Jump and Say Valentine's Day Is
For Kids Too!
Jump and Look For a Clue!
Jump and Say Happy Birthday to You!
Jump For Everything Blue!
Jump, Hop and Say Happy Easter To You!
Jump and Say Cock-A-Doodle-Do!
Jump and Sing Da-Do-Do-Do!
Jump and Ask Who? Who?
Jump and Squawk Like a Cockatoo!
Jump and Ask Is It You or Ewe?
Jump and Say There's an Ewww in My Stew!
Jump and Say Merry Christmas To You!
Jump and Cheer Happy New Year!
Jump and Say There's a Moo-Moo in a Tutu!
Jump and Say There's a Hare in My Hair!
Jump and Say My Aunt Ate An Ant!
Jump and Say There's An Aardvark
In The Amusement Park!

Jump and Roar For The Dinosaurs!
Jump and Buzz Like A Bee!
Jump and Flutter Like A Butterfly!
Jump and Pop Like Popcorn!

Clap For Series
Clap for 1!
Clap for 2!
Clap for 3!
Clap for 4!
Clap for 5!
Clap for 6!
Clap for 7!
Clap for 8!
Clap for 9!
Clap for 10!

The Cat Who Said Hello
The Three Boulders
Billy Shakespeare/Billie Shakespeare
Learn To Draw With Symmetry
ABC More Learn to Draw With Symmetry

Non-Fiction
103 Fundraising Ideas For Parent Volunteers With
Schools and Teams

www.ingramcontent.com/pod-product-compliance
Lightning Source LLC
Chambersburg PA
CBHW051247120626
46547CB00014B/1836